WHAT
WE
LOST
in the
SWAMP

— *poems* —

GRANT CHEMIDLIN

central
avenue

2023

Published by Central Avenue Publishing, an imprint of Central Avenue Marketing Ltd.
www.centralavenuepublishing.com

WHAT WE LOST IN THE SWAMP

Trade Paperback: 978-1-77168-289-3
EPUB: 978-1-77168-290-9

Published in Canada
Printed in United States of America

1. POETRY / LGBT   2. POETRY / Subjects & Themes - Nature

3 5 7 9 10 8 6 4

for my parents

I

WHEN I REALIZED I WAS A GREEN TREE FROG IN ANOTHER LIFE

It was a dark & rainy day in sixth-grade science
& the canary-colored light of the overhead projector

showed us picture after picture:
a montage of camouflaging creatures.

The name of the game was simple:
Who can find what's hiding in plain sight?

& I did. Every time. The only member
of our sleepy-eyed pride who could raise their hand

& give the answer. O their baffled eyes,
the looks of frustration on their flushed-red faces

when they couldn't understand the advantage
I had, how I knew all the tricks of the walking stick,

of the green tree frog & the phantom moth.
They begged & they begged for me to spill

my sacred secret (that I knew because I lived it).
Because prey sees prey, & I was keen

on all their cleverness, their tactics
to survive.

Take a closer look & see the seams
of my disguise:

the backwards ball cap, the Abercrombie clothes,
my use of "dude" in every sentence,

all just fabrics, a hand-stitched invisibility cloak
to hide the boy

who used to try on all his sister's
dresses,

who liked to play with dolls
when no one was around to stop him,

who wishes, now,
that when the teacher asked the final question,

he had pointed to himself.

I OFTEN FEEL

I often feel
the way a butterfly
flies:

chaotically,   moving too fast
to ever really see
clearly,

like a fighter jet   flailing,
that out of control,
engine lost,
nose-diving.

But then I land,   briefly,
& everything is still,
my wings
                included.

& there, right there,
in the daisy's
drop of dew,
I start
                to see it:

my vivid brightness,

before I'm off
again,
                tumbling,

a strange
                & stunning
violence
on
          the wind.

THE BOY & THE BLUE BIRD

I want to see your secrets,
the things you've hidden up high
& out of sight.

Little bird,
let my autumn shed your tree,
let me lay down its thistle crown
of crimson leaves.

I wish to see
                    your nest,

sacred chapel of twigs & grass,
the place you go
when you seek retreat
from song & sea-sky,

hidden home
in which you rest,
undress,
confess your sins
when no one else
is watching.

WHAT WE LOST IN THE SWAMP

Boys do not kiss boys. They catch frogs.
Is what I told myself the second it happened.

& there we were, hidden in the hemlocks of a secret swamp.
Your lips drifting away from mine like a silent ship

leaving harbor. Gone, as quickly as it came. I watched the shame
leap into the pond of your face. O the ripples.

How good we were at turning moments into paper,
into things we could crumple up & throw away.

You grabbed the frog squirming in my palms
& headed to the "cave," to the crack between the rocks,

where the black & white striped garter snake
slithered into shade. How I wish I could say

that I stopped you, that I didn't watch unhinged jaws
spring out like lightning, wrap around that poor

& unsuspecting frog, but I did.
Still too young to believe it, I wanted to see it

gone, eaten, that green & slippery part of myself
buried in the belly of a beast.

SLEEPLESS

I am a million trillion ants
trapped in a stretchy sack
of skin.

I am hip bones, wrestling
with every edge
they touch.

I can hear nothing,   now,
but the incessant, scratching
wind,

the rattling of the dusty fan
that spins & spins
& spins.

My muscles plucking
like a violent violin
whose flossy strings

are pulled so tight
they sing
their snapping songs.

I long
for comfort,
to lie upon this big Cal King

& flee
this tortured
            presence.

PORTRAIT OF MY MOTHER AS THE WIND

On the windiest of days, I learn to be grateful.

Like today, for instance,
I woke up a twisted pretzel
of anxiety,
my shrunken lungs gasping,
unable to breathe
through the squeeze
of stress.

But when I stepped
outside, the Wind, she supplied,
saying,

Here, take my air.
Let it fill your chest
with sweet, sunny swirls
of ocean sky.

Feel my breeze caress your skin.
Let every gust lift up your chin,
my way to say:

>   *You are alright,*
>   *that at its very core*
>   *life*
>   *is good*
>   *& kind*
>   *& beautiful.*

TO THE POPULAR KIDS WHO CALLED ME GAY

No, you never forget it:
when the archer nearly knocks

the red & fleshy truth
clean off your head.

That fruit,

that natural thing you've always felt
but won't believe.

O the balancing.
O the horror

if you turned
& saw it pinned against the tree

for the world to see.

Your secret,
dripping sweet with seeds,

the person whom you're meant to be
unleashed

without permission.

TO THE POPULAR KIDS WHO CALLED ME GAY (ABRIDGED)

You were right.

THE SWAN

Today, I'm feeling broken,   hollow,
jealous of the chimes outside,

                              so I swallow

wind,

        feel it tumble down my throat,
then listen

              to the dangled bones

                              moan.

Call me Snow White.

Call me Pied Piper

                  of the daytime crawlers.

My mouth   swings open
       & everything that sings,

                              I let inside:

the little hiding mice
        with their drumstick tails,

the woodpecker
         pecking at my heart,

the choir of crickets,
        the frogs with their ribbits,

the queen bees humming
        in my ears.

I do not blink.

I try my best   to hold my breath,
   to never swallow,

or all this life inside will die,

                              digest

into thick, bitter quiet.

Please, I beg.

       Don't leave me silent.
Don't let me be the swan

          without   a song.

THE LADYBUG

Is this how pathetic I've become?
Is this the extent of what rejection

does to a person? Is hitting rock
bottom when your heart gets broken

by a ladybug?

A ladybug who, during my walk,
refused to hop on my thumb?

Wouldn't move, wouldn't budge,
wouldn't waste those smooth,

those spotted wings on me.
Just crawled on her own,

undeterred by my attempts
to block her way,

so completely unafraid
to leave me lonely in the shade

as if she knows I'll be okay,
as if she knows one day

I'll see that strength is born
in moving forward.

THE STONER SAFARI

The troops had gathered in the backyard, one of those August
nights that's never really night, when the moon is so plump, so
ripe with light

that everything it touches stays alive, bright & sleepless.
We had a secret mission, a surprise place I wanted to show them,
& so, we began our long descent.

Jumped the fence, then crept through the silence
of the overgrown forest, thick with thistle, the tall, itchy crabgrass
slapping at our legs.

R was nervous, but J, in his lime green safari hat, couldn't stop
laughing at poor A, her flip-flops stuck, swallowed
by the quicksand-like mud.

I wouldn't let them give up. Guided by starlight, we scraped
& scratched & laughed our way through a final patch of thorns,
& then, we arrived:

a wide-open space, as far as the eye could see—an oasis
of sprawling golf course greens, drenched in dew & moon juice,
with nothing left to do

but run & scream at the top of our lungs. Press our lips
to a couple of thin, smoking spliffs & pretend like the night
would never end,

like it wasn't the cusp, the eve before the change, before we'd
separate & A would move into the city & J would leave to finish
school. & me,

I'd pack up my whole life in a single suitcase, fly across
the country to start all fresh & new, leaving baby brother R
to man our childhood bedroom

alone. I honestly can't recall what happened next,
but I like to think we started howling at the moon,
wild & freeing fire-breathing only youth can do, before

they forget.

THE PLEA

Here I am,
standing at the edge of the great cliff,
still waiting for the moment,
for the skies to rip open,
when the Universe
will pour down
from her heavenly house
& pronounce me ready,
unshroud
her many mysteries
of *how*,
of what it means
to be grown.
O Majesty, please!
Let me bow!
Let me bend my knee
so you, with your silver sword,
can knight me

Adult.

I wish to know,
to feel control,
to understand
the slipping sand
beneath my feet.

PORTRAIT OF A PAINTER PAINTING

What makes me a good writer
is how I can describe the dive off a cliff

a hundred different ways
without ever having done it.

How I can convince you a bolt of lightning
shot up through my stomach,

that the wind whipped my hair,
that those great big arms

of air, ancient & eager, grabbed my feet
to pull me faster.

How I'm plagued.

Good at writing doesn't mean
I am brave.

All I ever do is make the words
walk the plank, while I stay

dry.

At what point does art
stop imitating lies?

At what point does life
become a stencil?

When did all my lines
go gray, pencil-thin?

I'm starting to think
it doesn't matter

how I write,
how long I try

to color in, to shade
from a distance;

that no trick
of the light

will ever make
the untouched canvas

full.

DOG DAYS

For a while, I let my hands
do the seeing, the believing,

the backseat feeling
under gym shorts.

I guess I thought
if I could draw the line

at my wrist,
if I could wear it

like a bracelet,
then this, this kind

of primal touch,
could never be conceived

as something intimate,
could never be as unforgivable

as kissing, as hoping
that the jock

from down the block
knew my name.

How many games
did I play

alone?

How many thumb wars
did it take?

How many bones
did my dog days

hide in the dirt
before the fully formed

skeleton

rose on its own
& walked away?

II

LITTLE HYMN I

I drilled a hole
in my own heart.
I thought it'd ease
the swelling pain
of all these
feelings.

TOUCHDOWN

When I told my parents
I was dating a *he* instead
of a *she*, they were sitting
quietly in the living room,
eyes glued to a Notre Dame
football game. My mother
(as she always does) flooded
the room with a typhoon
of questions. While my
father, clearly not quite sure
yet how to handle the death
of an s, sat wordless, his face
frozen.
Although he did not move,
I watched him slip away,
crawl through the screen
of the TV, into the safety
of the bleachers packed
with roaring fans. The scene
became a picture,
a *Where's Waldo?*,
a collage of fathers
hiding in the stands.

SPLASH

I want to be original.

I want to be the guy that made the first
baked potato.

The mom
who accidentally dropped an Oreo
in milk & called it genius.

I want you speechless.

I want to do my latest trick.

I want to show you all the ways
I can bend
                    this paper clip

into something new, something different.

Look, earrings! Look, tiny spear for small fishing!

For finger food, fingers fighting.

Bow your thumb
& watch me
                    knight him.

Yes,

I want to be original

but not because I want to throw something back
into the river,

not because I want a little piece of me
to float downstream,

to join
the collective thoughts
swimming.

No,

I'm crass.

I want my recognition
singular.

I want to catch your eye,
make a splash

just big enough
for you

to look my way,

see me standing
all aglow.

I want to be original,

which is a fancy
way to say

that I don't want to be invisible

                              to you,

anymore.

MY FIRST DATE WITH ANOTHER MAN WAS

Awkward.

The two of us, like little teacups
still fresh from the cupboard,
sitting across from one another
without a clue of what to do
or how to act. Me, with my ball cap,
I tried to read this Cali surfer bro,
but the swelling in my throat became
distracting. How uncomfortable
we must have seemed, the two of us
still holding our own internalized
homophobia like great big onions
in our hands, hovering, both
scared of the stench, of the sour, stinging
eyes those layered lies could bring.

By the end, I knew he liked me,
not because he told me, or passionately
kissed me. (He did neither.) It was when
he walked me to my car, how he stopped
to sheepishly ask
if we could take another lap
around the block.

FLOAT

Like you / my social anxiety / ability to connect with people

always manifests itself / as gravity / messing with me

in every room / I go into / Every party / gathering

always starts / for me / with reeling / this feeling

that isn't floating / but a sinking / up / People talking

on the ground / & I'm walking / on / the ceiling

Yes / it's hard / to make new friends / while upside down

Hard / when everyone / just thinks / I'm frowning

But tonight / you sail / into the room

shoes off / dancing / in the chandelier's / gold hue

a spinning top / & everything / I see / goes

right side up / We never say a word / take our seats

on the ceiling fan / whirring / laughing / without a care

for those below.

I FEEL BAD FOR ALL THE STRAIGHT MEN

I feel bad for all the straight men
that have never experienced

an orgasm
from prostate   stimulation.

I feel bad
because they don't know what they're missing,

because theirs can only be
a simulation

compared to mine, this divine
fine wine & fruit basket.

Draw them like your French girls, Jack.
Draw them naked, unafraid,

empathetic.

Let them see the straight edge
                                    bent.

Let them see what strength
can really look like,

warm wax pouring
over every single organ

in their bodies,
them savoring

the slow
& graceful scrape.

Paint the world
a safer place.

Show the way to swallow pride
& ride

the earthquake.

WARNING OF A WINTER STORM

It is snowing somewhere in this godforsaken country.
I sense it. I feel the fangs of cold frisk my skin,

even though I'm standing, sweating like a scorched piece
of street meat in the California sun.

Call it *brethren*. Call it *desperate connection to the winter storm.*

How quickly I ignore the reports, the weather warnings,
the pitiful fact: it's been three weeks since you last

called me back & I am nothing,   really,

just a single flake of snow
making my way through the blizzard in your brain,

delicately drifting in the whipping wind of pain
like all the others:

the cold, hopeless souls
that will never know   the real you,

only grow

                to love

                        the falling.

LETTER TO MY PAST-LIFE LOVER

You deserved my words,
a conversation,
even if the explanation
crumbled from my mouth
like loose-leaf teeth,
the kind you see
in nightmares.
At least then,
you could have sorted through
the piles at your feet,
flipped & rearranged
my Scrabble squares
into something you could read,
a glimpse into sincerity,
my puzzle-piece apology.
But no,
I let fear zip my lips,
leaving you to view my silence
as *I guess he never cared.*
But I swear
that isn't true,
that our time was not some lie.
I didn't fake my feelings.
I was just confused,
lost in the fog
between who
I thought I had to be
& the man
I really am.

I'm sorry.

For hurting you,
confusing you,
leaving you
to question
every second ever spent,
every word I ever said;
that I used
three thousand miles

to excuse
myself
from the table talk
we both know
you
deserved.

THE WEAK BEAK BRINGS FEATHERS

The birds are circling again
& I hate it—

their flocking, their squawking,
their watching me watch them.

The thought is unnerving:

how we, the lucky, living things,
always swirl & surround

something dying.

I know for most a flapping wing
is just goodbye, a quiet celebration,

but I have seen (up close)
how death can devolve

even the best of us
into a vulture-blooded breed.

Those
who do not view the glide as grief

but a twirl
before

the taking.

I STILL HEAR YOU IN THE RAIN

My grandmother always gave such strange advice.
Her words—a cryptic, mystic Rubik's Cube
for a child's mind.

I remember once, her telling me
I should live my life like a light rain,
the kind you never notice
looking out from inside.

Now at the time
(I will admit), I didn't get it.
But years have passed
& she is gone
& I am here,
squinting out an old bay window,
finally seeing through all of my missing,
the droplets of rain:

there all along,

quietly constant,
growing the ground
for all those around it,
never needing
to be seen,
only hoping
to be felt.

PORTRAIT OF A PLANT ON FIRE

M came back from the hardware store today
with a big bag of soil. & when I asked
what he was up to, he gestured to the dying fern
in the corner, how its long & fan-like leaves
had turned pale yellow, spotted & droopy.
I watched with fascination—his caring hands
as they cupped the spidered roots, lifted up
that hopeless little fern from its hollow crimson
home. Right then, I could see it: the slightest smile
spreading on his face as he replaced that dry,
that useless dirt with layer after layer
of new & fertile fluff. Is this not the perfect image
of true love? Of what life can be boiled down to
in a bright red pot? The very core of all our hopes:
that someone, someday, will come along in our most
dire moments of need, of feeling lonely,
& feed us a fresh, an unconditional love.

FOR THE LOVE OF DUSK I

Four o'clock
& the garden starts growing dark,
a November sun's curtain call.
Dusk is coming.

I look
to the very tops of the trees,
still sun-soaked,
orange autumn leaves
ablaze.
This is our time, they say.
You'll get more tomorrow.

& even though
I stand in shadow,
I accept
& I smile,
unwilling to act
like the spoiled youngest child.

I know my place,
that the special bond
between
sun & tree
long precedes me.

HOW THE HOME SAYS HELLO

Today, for the very first time,
I met my home,
even though I've lived here since May.

I can't quite say what came over me
(perhaps a need for answers, for comfort,
some sign from the Universe that I'll be okay),
but early this morning,
before the birds or the boys had awoken,
I decided to lie on the living room floor
& this time,
                listen,   *really listen*
to the silence, to the overture of quiet
I hadn't let myself feel
                      before.
Then it happened:
the groan of cedar planks,
scratching wind against the panes,
the tick, tick, tick,
& echoed drips from rusted pipes,
all the cracks & creaks coming to life
& I swear I could feel it—
the giant, beating heart beneath
the hardwood.

BEFORE WE SLEEP, WE BATHE IN THE RIVER

It is silly time
in bed again,

those last & precious
minutes of the day

we spend

flapping around
like two fish out of water.

Me, wrapped in seaweed,
I can hear you laughing

at my loud & guttural
otter sound. Smiling,

because you know those
primal shouts

are signs
of my uncontrollable love,

of a dam done breaking,
of a man washed clean,

so completely
himself

when around you.

III

LITTLE HYMN II

The world

is a pearl

on your tongue.

TOUR DE FORCE

I like to think we inherit more than looks,
that *loves* are passed down just as easily.

I know for me, I got my father's
love of weather. I still remember,
growing up, anytime it would storm,
how we'd dress in our boots & our coats,
how we'd pile in his car & he'd drive us around
& we'd watch as the wind worked her magic.
I always loved it. The excitement,
the rush & the gush of it all,
how once-waning streams would roar into life,
into rivers, into seas we could name,
how the streets became moats,
every car a slick boat,
fallen trees—prickled beasts we'd slain.

It was a father's gift of awe & wonder,
a deeply profound respect for Mother Nature.
It is why anytime I hear a patter on our roof,
I grab your hand & rush outside
to make you dance beneath the downpour,

our splashing boots, our beating hearts
in tune with all that thunder.

THE DRESSMAKER

When we met
I was dressed in rags & filth.
I didn't know how to sew
a single seam.

But you, homemaker,
master dressmaker,
sat me down
& showed me how
to make a stitch,
how to take
my inexperience
& twist it
into thread.

Such beaded brilliance!
The way you wrap our souls
in glitter & gold,
how you can sew a house
into a home,
take two fabrics,
separate & full,
& weave them together
as a bigger, better

whole.

THE GARDEN GATE

I have been into the weeds
                  & seen it.

The slight,   nondescript   & paper thin

difference   between confidence

& feeling good enough.

Will I ever have the latter? I always ask,
or does this ladder never end?

                 Step   after step   after
step

until I'm seasick,   swaying up high in the deep blue
sky
full of wind
        & nothingness.

I want to be so many things   in my life
I've made a list:

Soft as the fuzzy cattail's tip;

             brave as the bracing, pin-thin nail,
             always standing up
               to the hammer's

heavy hit.

I want to feel at home   everywhere I go
like the slow-moving snail;

          a sand crab,   fast
& uncatchable,
            forever leaving me
              squatting
at the water's edge,

believing in a new
      & beachy magic.

I know this will sound strange,
but most of all,

      I want to be the garden gate,

not the tall & steely wall   out front   that opens
on its own,

but the old & wooden thing   out back
with the little black metal latch

that always moans   at the feeling   of your hands.

Maybe that is all   it really takes,

feeling good enough for you,   because of you,

your gentle touch,   & the rest

      just falls

      into place.

THE WAYS I PHOTOSYNTHESIZE

I have written a to-do list

where every slot is filled

with *Notice*,
           with *Watch*, with *Listen*.

So here I am, in the living room,

           once again trying my best

to crawl through the cracks of this world,

    to be small & see big,

feel the spider's
          silver string,

              how it sways

between us,   between everything.

& then I notice

how for one fleeting hour,

           the plants in the corner

    get their light.

Sun, beaming bright,

       a single, godly spotlight

come to save them.

& I can't help but smile,
           greet them

       like they're next of kin, like somehow

I can see myself

     in the flowers,

         their potted roots, my own.

You see,
     all day I wither till I'm home,

till I'm next to you,

     till we're cocooned

         in colorful quilts

sprawled out on our couch,

   where I lie in your light,

soak my skin,
     bask
        in your warm & golden

till slowly,

     once again,
         I come alive.

THE SOMETIMES-JEALOUS GUY

I am so mad at you when I wake up from this dream
that I want to scream, that I want to shake you from your deep

& distant slumber to demand some semblance of an answer.
How could you? How could you sit in that dark sailors' bar

with my nemesis & laugh (LAUGH) at all his useless starfish
jokes? How could you go behind my back & massage

his meaty calves with all your strength? Did you forget that that's
our thing? That all those young & impressionable seashells

were watching? How could you? How could you let his disgusting
crab claws pinch your perfect speckled cheeks? I won't

believe it. My lying eyes: You, putting down your spaghetti
to stand & check his head for lice. Is there anything

more intimate? Or how about next, when you together
started naming all the mice that scurried by?

Fiona. Mr. Billy. Wet Willy. Princess Di.

No, no, of course, I'll never say out loud that I'm
a sometimes-jealous guy. It's just my mind, it runs quite wild,

being blessed (but also stricken) with this vast (& sometimes rash)
imagination.

THE LITTLE BUILDER MAN

Anytime my lover & I
get into a (very rare) fight
& it's my fault, my anger, my doing,
the little builder man inside my throat
unfurls,
           walks around in circles,
stomping his feet,
              reciting my apology.
It goes like this for hours: constant chattering
so I can't read, can't sleep, can't think
about anything
                but
                    the inevitable.

It's his way of making sure I know
I cannot sit & sulk
                forever,
that when the necessary silence
has passed,
the distance done, I will have
to open my mouth
                to let him out,
                to fix the bridge
                              I broke.

SALLY (WHEN THERE'S NOTHING LEFT TO SELL)

Plants in Los Angeles look like coral,
like seaweed, which is another way to say

that every time I'm walking down the street,
I'm underwater. Look at that bush over there

with its long, pipe cleaner limbs, like a spindly green
octopus. *How'd you get so deep down here?* he asks,

but I'm too busy looking up at the surface,
minding my silence, wondering why every note

that dives below sounds muted, wondering
how something as violent as drowning,

as sinking to the bottom, from above
looks peaceful, looks small, looks

practically invisible to the flock of gulls
passing by.

DIE HARD

Over dinner, you ask me how my day went
& I explain how at work today, I shrank down

to the size of a push pin,
followed an absurd & scrambling line of ants

to their crack in the curb. You say,
Why do you always make yourself so small?

When you really mean, *Why do you hate yourself?*
Is this somehow my fault?

I say, *Don't you know how many secret cities I've seen?*
When I really mean, *This is my escape. This is how I've learned*

to flee. My whole life, I've had a fear of changing heights,
issues fitting into lunchrooms & friend groups.

I call it Alice Syndrome, how a swallowed secret
can either make a person small (& unseen) or so tall

they're bursting through the roof.
Maybe you were right & old habits die hard.

Maybe I was wrong & I haven't grown at all.
Maybe I'll admit that there are things

I can work on, things that now I promise
I will work on.

51

HOLY SIGNS OF THE CRACKED & CRUMBLED COOKIE

Why is it the most obvious things in the world
are the hardest to believe? Hardest to keep close,

keep clung to the bones? Why does it take a miracle
for me to finally see the truth?

If I say it, oh, no, no, I certainly won't believe it.
& if you say it, most trusted, love of my life,

I think you're lying, conspiring against me.
But if I hear it whispered in the wind,

if the birds start to sing, if the clouds form a shape,
a godly sign, if all my favorite stars align, then

I'll listen. I'll let it stick because it's mystic,
a twist of fate, a brush with luck, with wonder.

& you know this.

It is why the other night, when I had once again
tumbled down the well beneath our bed, skipped dinner

because I couldn't stop going on about the writing on the wall,
how it said I was nothing, a no one, a failure,

you handed me a sign:

an unwrapped fortune cookie, come to turn my tides.
Of course, I wouldn't realize

till later, but the entire time I was sulking,
upset about my writing,

you were tweezing in the kitchen, carefully replacing
the message from inside with your own slip of white.

Do it because you love it,

it reads & these are the things you are willing
to do for me. Your love & your light so bright, so brave

you would fight the Fates if it meant I'd be safe,
bring forth your own divine holy sign

so that I'll listen, so I'll feel relief, so all those silly,
obvious things,

               they stay.

SIT.

Today, my therapist tells me I need to   *retrain my brain.*
So of course, I dive deep
                              into a metaphor.

It looks like this:

Me, coming home to a scratching at the door.
I open wide & there's my mind—a wild mess.

Can you picture it?

          a brain
                    with four shaggy legs?
                    a happy tail, hot puppy breath?

I pick him up. I pat his head.
& then I see
              the damage:

                    how once again, he tipped the can
                         & rummaged through the darkness,

                    jumped onto the countertop
                         & ate my plate of confidence.

                    Of course, the tracked-in trails of doubt
                         he smeared all across

. . . *the carpet?*   (my therapist gently
                                   interjects).

This is all great, Grant. All wonderfully   in-depth.

But tell me what you do. Tell me, what happens next?

               I scream.

                         I curse.

I start to blame,

but all I hear   is

                        must retrain

         is   *don't feel shame.*

So I go.

You go?

                     Yes, I take some space.

Then when I'm back,
I put in place
           a fresh pee-pad,
                  a training crate.

(She laughs.) *Because?*

I won't give up.

One day,
         this loud, disruptive pup,
             he'll learn to sit,
             he'll know to stay,

& the silly sign upon my face,

               the one that reads   *Beware of Brain,*

will finally have

        no use.

THE HUFF & PUFF OF ME

When my brain is stuck
in a negative rut,
I am a force
of self-
destruction,
a howling wind
that rips through towns
to blow
every thin
straw house down.

But while I topple,
twirl & heave,
your stubborn brick bones
never leave.
I'm here, you say,
through thick & thin,
through tidal waves,
through violent winds.
I'll never let you feel alone.
Crawl in my heart
& make your home.

GOLD DOG TAG

The other day I was walking back from lunch
when a woman approached me,
asking if I'd seen her gold dog tag.
It must've fallen off on our morning walk, she said.
Will you please keep an eye out as you go?

So I smiled & agreed & continued on my way,
but my eyes would not lift up from that street.
They were scanning every rock, every crack
& blade of grass. I was obsessed.
Compulsively, I felt this need to find it:
a thing that wasn't mine, for a dog I didn't know.

& even though I (of course) never found it,
the moment left me thinking,
left me wishing I could split in two,
walk up to myself on a similar sunny day
& say, *Hey. I think I dropped my confidence
a few blocks back. Have you seen it?*

'Cause maybe then I'd try my best,
search high & low, become obsessed
with sailing every sea until I felt like
me again.

SPACE WALKS

(I will whisper this to ensure it does not set in stone.)

It's becoming increasingly clear
I may never go to space
to fulfill my dream of exploration.

So instead I pretend,

settling for walks around my town,
small tours of a neighborhood nebula.
I like to think about the self-contained, boxy Milky Ways
inside each house, all those swirling worlds
that pay no mind to the things outside their orbit.

How many passing planets teem with life?
How many on the brink of extinction?
Now show me those who live & grow despite
the approaching asteroid.

TROUBLES

I couldn't escape it:
the deep-seated,
paranoid thought,
the *what-if,*
the *maybe it's not*
working
after all.
Even as I stood
in the kitchen
boiling
a pot
of water
for our pasta,
I could feel
that I was being
watched:
an unfriendly monster,
submerged subconscious
simmering beneath
the surface
with its million wary eyes,
bubbles full of pupils,
black
& unblinking.

IV

LITTLE HYMN III

If there really is
a god
up there,
I hope she'll answer
just one
prayer.

Please,
oh lord,
persuade me to
believe
not in you
but myself.

THE YEAR I VOLUNTEERED AT A HOSPICE CARE

I visited _____ again today.
(The empty space because legally,
I cannot give the name of a person in hospice.)

What I can say, though,
is how beautifully strange it is
to sit with someone dying,

how every sunny Sunday
I come to read her poems,
play her music from my phone,
but mostly, I'm there
to hold the space,
her hand, if heavy eyes decide
to weep or sleep.

She cannot speak
or understand the words I say,
so the only things I know about her
are her name, her age, the fact
that she is dying.

It sounds so strange,
but it took until today's visit
for me to finally realize
that could be the most
I ever get.

I will probably never know
her favorite color, favorite food,
all the places she's been to,
if she likes to dance
& if she does, with whom?

How did you meet the love of your life?
I whisper into the ether,
as if my softer tone might work,
might slip those words
beneath the closed door between us.

Of course, I never get an answer,
but I take in all the things I can:
long silver hair,
crooked bottom teeth,
how her sea-green eyes
seem to smile back at me.

I'm well aware this final page
is all I'll read, but if I just capture
all these smaller things,
the bits & pieces I can see,
if heaven's a collection
of other people's memories,
then hers, hers will be
a little bigger.

LIVING ROOM WITH A VIEW

When you look out our front bay window
(the one that streams),   all you see
is green:

the many emerald leaves of the tall hedge wall
that surrounds us,

the lime, the pickle, the deep seaweed
of the succulents sprouting by the fountain.

Of course, I'd be remiss if I didn't mention
the towering beauty of the single cypress tree.

Its sage & slender silhouette
the only thing you can see

                    beyond the wall.

I have yet to decide
whether or not I think it's possible to fall

in love with a color,
with its many faces, the protection it provides.

You see, it's all those looming   *other times,*
afternoons when I am looking out

& cannot tell the feeling, cannot decipher
whatever's teetering beneath my skin,

when the comfort turns to question:
Is this safe? Or am I

            caged within the hedge maze?

HOW THE CONSTELLATIONS CAN SAVE US

Does the sin stay?

burning ball & chain

a sun in the sky that won't set?

Always hot & harsh
              & unforgiving,

so anywhere we go in life
              is blistering,

so everything we touch
              melts our skin?

What if,

          instead of drought,

instead of pain

        & endless days

           of scorched flesh, regret,

we saw our sins
           not as suns,

but as stars in the night?

Distant fixtures

         of things forgiven,

flickers

      we cannot move or undo

but use
         to find our way.

THE QUIET HOUR

I like to spend my mornings
reading by the streaming window,
teakwood lit, sipping on espresso.

It's my happy place,
those precious, final seconds,
that sliver of space
between morning & commute
when I blow out the candle, when I put on my shoes,
look up to see that the whole world has paused,
willed me the chance to stop & watch
the smoke
        as it swirls in the light.

I know that I am lucky
never to have seen a person die
but today, I find myself thinking,

Wouldn't it be nice if this were what we saw?

If, when the stubborn wick was snuffed
(before grief arrived),
we received this token of hope:
to see the soul rise,
        twirl up from the body,
so gracefully
      dance, expand, then disappear into the air
all around us.

What reassurance that would be,
to know
    that even when they left,
when they couldn't be seen,
still,
    we breathed them in.

THE BREAKING

How do I do it? How do I do it gently? Lovingly?
What is the careful way to go about the breaking
of your heart? One that isn't smashing, that isn't
sneak attack, that isn't opening the kitchen cabinet
just to watch the shelf snap, just to watch the stacks
of bowls & fancy dinner plates slip, cascade down
to the cold, relentless floor—a roaring porcelain
waterfall. I want *humane*. I want something that doesn't end
in drowning, the pain of two shattered tongues.
Wasn't it you who said that love is like a living,
breathing thing? That ours sleeps, curled up,
at the foot of our bed? Maybe you were wrong
& I'm a coward, selfish. Maybe I was right
that you're too stubborn, blinded. Maybe this is asking
way too much, but can't the two of us put down our love
like an old family dog? Can't we just sit there, together,
side by side, holding it, stroking it, consoling it
(& one another)? Because we know that it is time,
that this is right, that neither of us will ever have
another love quite like this, but it has suffered enough,
has run its course, so now the feeble fur must rest.
& when the overly peppy vet tech raises her head
to tell us that it's passed, we can hug. We can exchange
sad smiles & with our heavy hearts full of fond,
mostly happy memories, we can leave. We can go
our separate ways having felt the peaceful way
to break.

MEET & GREET

I asked
& he agreed.

So here I am now,
sitting at the coffee shop

down the street,
patiently waiting

to meet parallel universe
me.

The one that didn't move
across the country,

the one that said he'd stay
east,

the one that gets to see his family
every weekend, holiday,

gets to teach his baby nephew
how to swim

when the pool
gets opened.

I want to see how he turned out,
if this version of myself

still makes it out
of the closet.

If he does
& now

he's stronger,
happier than me.

I want to fill the little hole
inside my chest

that keeps on leaking
the constant sand

that won't stop spilling.
The all-night thinking

of these lives
I used to know

but now
I don't.

Living through
the phone

can never really count
as making memories,

can only ever be
a Dalí painting:

something unreal,
something melting.

The barista tops me off
& now the sinking hands

of the clock
start singing.

In my booth,
I keep on thinking

how every answer
that I want,

I know will show
if he just

doesn't.

LIVING ROOM LILIES

How strange, I think
as I sit sipping in my kitchen,

watching dawn slowly slither in
through the cracks of another

sleepless night.

How I try
for stillness,

but can only feel the world
spinning

beneath my feet,

can only see
the quiet symbols of my life

changing
in the early amber light.

Living room lilies
that used to stand

for beauty,
unfurling,   now,

with grief.

POCKETS

I found a watch today that I thought I lost
two years ago. Bamboo face, light leather strap,
just sitting in my backpack. I laugh
because it's been here all along, tucked
in a tiny side pocket, walking everywhere
I walk, the complete & utter opposite
of lost, of loss. I used to wear it every day.
I used to feel naked without it. I used to
love to show it off, but this time when I
put it on, when it's finally reunited with
my wrist, it all feels different. Like the
lightness I used to brag about to friends
is gone. Like isn't it funny how time makes
everything feel heavy? Actually, I change
my mind. Maybe this isn't the opposite
of loss, but a synonym. Maybe everything
we think is gone is just unseeable, is just
hiding, is just inside, twisted in the fabrics
of our lives, walking everywhere we walk.

DEAR C,

What is it with this cat & windows?
                    I want to call him *Lord of the Threshold. Crowned*
Feline of Outside
Watching.

I wish you were here right now. I wish you could have seen
how he leaped
                    six, maybe seven feet
                                into the air, all to reach
a simple square
of light.

                    What does he see out there
                                        that I don't?
I have to ask myself,

amazed by his amazement, his fearlessness,
          how everything
                    is worth the risk,
                                worth falling, worth
getting hurt if it means
he could catch a glimpse,
                    if it means he could sniff the air,
                                                    feel
the coolness

on his fur—so soft & soothing it moves
like a river through your hands.

                    I bet one pet & you'd be cured,
                                        brain reborn,
                    baptized
in the curling black & gray.

I'm starting to believe that pain is not a solid wall,
                                        but glass,

something to see through, something to show you
                                there is beauty on
the other side.

I know that one day soon,
            he & I will be sitting on the floor
by the big bay window,
                        watching as the mother birds
flutter by, as they hide

in the sanctum of our green & leafy hedge
        & there you'll be,

turning the corner,   waving

as you walk up to our door.

ROOTS

Nature vs. Nurture.

      Man vs. Man

            vs. Plant.

I hear their laughter

          blooming in the highest

of their branches.

        Sure disaster,

           one oak whispers,

how they act as if us trees will not

            outlive them,

how they think we cannot speak,

         how they choose to never see

the roots connected.

FOR THE LOVE OF DUSK II

Back East,
dusk looks different,
better than I remember.
The autumn sky—
a chilly silver screen
of film noir,
full of mystery,
of romance
between fleeting light
& the silhouettes
of branches.

I breathe in brisk air
& receive
at this secret meeting
of the trench coat trees,
a coded message:

remember the beauty
that's forgotten,
the little things
we leave behind
anytime
our road diverges.

SANDBOX

I miss the bliss
of ignorance,
the carefree days
of youthful play,
digging holes
in search of gold,
sculpting castles
from my mounds
of endless time.

How fast
the sandbox turns
into
an hourglass.
But I
am stubborn.
I will build
& I will play,
as long as this sinking sand
will have me.

MY BROTHER,

if all else fails,
if every last tomato plant
in the garden
shrivels up,
if we have nothing
but ourselves,

promise me
you'll be out front

where the lawn meets the street,
where the two leaning tree trunks
twist into one;

that if I'm brave enough
this time
to climb as high as you,
you'll be there

waiting

to hoist me up
that final branch,
to share the sunset view.

LETTER TO MY FORMER SELF

I'm the kind of guy
        who listens to rain
                on a clear day.

You're the kind of guy
        who's always rainbows
                & butterflies

        (decaying
                on the inside).

I'm the kind of guy
        who watches *Hocus Pocus*
                in July,

        who catches flies
                & lets them go,

        who likes the smell
                of fresh-laid mulch.

You're the kind of guy
        who thinks of death
                instead of growth,

        who thinks of dirt
                as something chewed

                        & someday you.

You're the kind of guy
        who always paints the roses red,
                while I paint blue.

You're the kind of guy
        who always does the things he's told.

                        I live my truth.

THE WAGON GAME

That smell of summer rain on asphalt
brings me back to the days of the wagon game.

Our four little bodies packed like sardines
in that red-green bin, teetering at the top

of our driveway. How the wheels gave slowly,
our tiny toes gnawed on by gravity,

how whoever sat in front had the immense
responsibility of steering, of guiding us down

the steep terrain. Captain who had to make
the impossibly sharp right turn to the front walk,

to the safety of the lawn, where of course
we'd tip & fall

again & again & again.

It was this fun, unruly ritual—our summer
ceremony—that unknowingly prepared us

for the uncertain future, for the inevitable
crashes & burns of life.

Because even today, when I spin out,
when I lose control & tumble down

into the grass, I can feel that same laughter
swelling in my chest,

like a silly made-up children's game
has somehow

given me the strength
to wipe the green off my jeans

& go again.

ACKNOWLEDGMENTS

Thank you to the editors at *Arlington Literary Journal* for publishing "When I Realized I Was a Green Tree Frog in Another Life" and to the editors at *ALOCASIA* for publishing "Portrait of a Plant on Fire" and "Sally (When There's Nothing Left to Sell)."

Thank you to the entire Central Avenue team for making this book the best it could be. Michelle, Beau, Jessica, Molly, I am forever indebted.

I am incredibly grateful to my friends and family who have supported my poetry journey over the last few years. Mom, Dad, Conor, Blair, Reid, you have been the greatest, most loving family a queer kid could ask for. Caitlin, oh my goodness Caitlin, my partner-in-poetry, I am so lucky to have you in my life. Thank you for always giving me your honest feedback. You know my poems better than I do sometimes.

Finally, to my husband, Brian. Thank you for your unwavering love, for believing in me even when I don't, and for allowing me the space to be my weirdest, most authentic self. I love you.

Photo: Eve Hinz

Grant Chemidlin is a queer poet and, currently, an MFA candidate at Antioch University Los Angeles. He is the author of the chapbook *New in Town* (Bottlecap Press, 2022) and the illustrated collection *He Felt Unwell (So He Wrote This)*. He's been a finalist for the Gival Press Oscar Wilde Award, the Philip Levine Prize for Poetry, and *Atlanta Review*'s International Poetry Contest. Recent work has appeared or is forthcoming in *Quarterly West, Iron Horse Literary Review, Tupelo Quarterly,* and *Saranac Review*, among others.

@grantcpoetry